Pal Has H<

by Sarah Curran   illustrated by Jo Brown

SCHOOL PUBLISHERS

ISBN 10 0-15-364056-1
ISBN 13 978-0-15-364056-8

1 2 3 4 5 6 7 8 9 10   179   17 16 15 14 13 12 11 10 09 08

Ordering Options
ISBN 10 0-15-364157-6
ISBN 13 978-0-15-364157-2

Lil has one big ham.

Bill has one big pot.

Bill can fill the pot.

See the big pot hiss!

Bill has ham.

Lil has ham.

Pal has a big ham.

School-Home Connection Have your child read the book to you. Then discuss what foods your family can prepare together.

Pal Has Ham
Word Count: 34

High-Frequency Words
one
see
the

Decodable Words*

a	**has**
big	**hiss**
Bill	**Lil**
can	**Pal**
fill	pot
ham	

Boldface words indicate sound-spelling introduced in this story.